INTO THE ABYSS

A Tour of Inner Space

by

Ellen Hopkins

Perfection Learning®

Cover design and inside layout: Michelle Glass

About the Author

Ellen Hopkins lives with her family, four dogs, two cats, and three tanks of fish near Carson City, Nevada. A California native, Ellen moved to the Sierra Nevada to ski. While writing for a Lake Tahoe newspaper, she discovered many exciting things and fascinating people.

Dedication

To my two moms: Toni, who created me, and Valeria, who pointed me in the right direction

Acknowledgment

Steve Etchemendy and the Monterey Bay Aquarium Research Institute

Cover Image: www.photodisc.com

Image Credits: photo by **Marv White** ©1996 MBARI p. 46; **M. Leet for MBARI** ©1997 p. 49; **Navy News Service** p. 4 (bottom); ©**Bettmann/CORBIS** p. 21 (top), 27 (bottom), 34, 42; ©**Reuters New Media Inc./CORBIS** p. 23 (photo); **Grumpy Partnership** pp. 29–30;

Inside Illustration: Kay Ewald pp. 9, 13, 15, 16; Larry Nolte p. 14; Michelle Glass pp. 7, 8

ArtToday (some images copyright www.arttoday.com); **Corel Professional Photos** pp. 11, 37, 45, 62, 64; **ISMI® Master Photos** p. 5; **NOAA** p. 23 (line art); **North Wind Picture Archives** pp. 24, 25, 26, 56; **Eyewire** p. 55; **Corel.com** p. 58

TABLE OF CONTENTS

INTRODUCTION
AN ALIEN WORLD

One dark night, Carole Richards took a walk along Malibu Beach. Suddenly, her little dog barked and charged ahead. Carole jogged after it. Abruptly, she stopped and screamed.

A 50-foot long *something* lay dead in the sand. It looked like a snake. Only it had a scarlet **dorsal** fin and a feathery red headdress. Was the bizarre beast from outer space?

No, it wasn't from outer space. But it was from "inner" space. The alien creature came from the mysterious world deep beneath the waves.

This creature was an oarfish. The name comes from the way its fins rotate like oars. People first discovered the odd fish in 1771. Since then, these fish have been spotted only about 25 times.

Scientists think this rare species lives in the great depths of the ocean. But they don't know much more. Oarfish may be moving toward **extinction**. Or maybe they're thriving, down in the ocean's deepest reaches. Down in a place called the **abyss**.

The *abyss* is an alien world full of alien creatures. Let's take a tour.

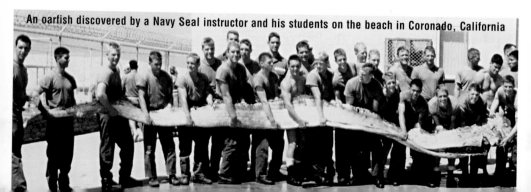

An oarfish discovered by a Navy Seal instructor and his students on the beach in Coronado, California

OUR WATERY WORLD

Before we set sail, let's learn a little about our watery world. The person who named our planet "Earth" was clueless. Of course, that was a very long time ago. He couldn't have known that almost ¾ of the earth lies underwater. A better name for our wet planet might have been "Blue."

Earth is unique. No other planet in our solar system looks the same. Nor do any have the same qualities.

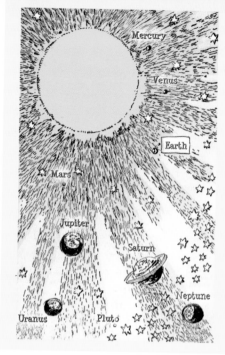

Most of the other planets are farther away from the sun than the earth is. So they are very cold. These planets might have water. But it would all be frozen.

Mercury and Venus are closest to the sun. They are very hot. Water on those planets would boil away.

Mars has a little water. But nothing like an ocean has been discovered there.

Water covers 71 percent of our planet. That's 140 million square

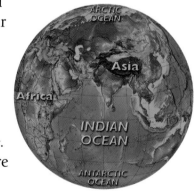

miles of the earth's surface covered by water. The "deep" (water that is at least 1 mile deep) covers 60 percent of the earth's surface. The average depth of all the earth's water is about 2½ miles.

Continents and undersea mountains divide our watery world. Three main divisions are the Atlantic, Pacific, and Indian Oceans. In the far south, these oceans join to form the Antarctic Ocean. Greenland, Europe, Canada, and Asia border the nearly circular Arctic Ocean in the north. With their gulfs and smaller seas, these five oceans form a chain of blue.

The earth's surface temperatures are just right to keep water wet. And the oceans cool the earth in summer and warm it in winter. It's amazing, when you think about it.

All of this water is good for the creatures that call Earth home. Every living thing needs water. In fact, the human body is made up of 70 percent water!

Seawater plays an important role in many of the earth's cycles. It **evaporates**. Then it rises to form clouds. And what goes up must come down. In this case, what comes down is rain. Without rain, we'd dry up and blow away.

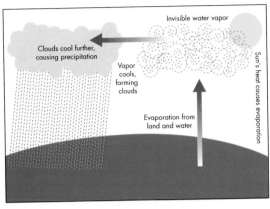

The air we breathe is made up of oxygen, nitrogen, and other gases. All animals need oxygen. Once air is inhaled, body cells use the oxygen. Carbon dioxide, or CO_2, is then exhaled as waste. Plants take in the CO_2 from the air and give back oxygen.

The same gasses are dissolved in seawater. Sea animals breathe dissolved oxygen. Marine plants use dissolved carbon dioxide.

MINERALS

Seawater also contains dissolved minerals and salts. How salty is seawater? The average salt content is 3.5 percent.

Some salt comes from rocks beneath the seafloor. Most comes from **eroding** mountains above the water's surface. As mountains crumble, they release minerals, such as salt. Rainwater washes these chemicals into the ocean.

Freshwater freezes at 32°F. But even frigid Arctic temperatures can't freeze seawater. It is too salty. Near the North and South Poles, some surface water does freeze. When this happens, extra salt is left behind. The water becomes even heavier.

MOTION

Polar water is very cold, very salty, and very heavy. It sinks as it gets heavier. Deeper, fresher water is forced up. This upward water movement is called *upwelling*. Upwelling is only one way seawater moves.

The ocean is in constant motion. To understand why, let's look at how the earth moves.

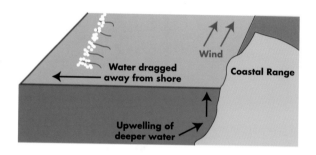

As the earth circles the sun, it tilts. The ocean gets more direct sun near the equator than at the poles because of the angle. As water warms, it expands. That makes the **sea level** higher at the equator than at the poles.

Seawater follows this slight downhill slope from the equator to the poles. As the water nears the poles, it cools. Once it reaches the poles, this colder, heavier water sinks. It spreads along the bottom and pushes cooler water toward the

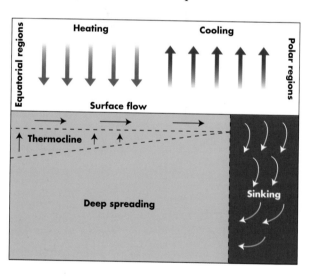

equator where it warms again. This exchange is called *thermohaline circulation*.

The Coriolis effect is another force that influences wind and ocean currents. North of the equator, the water spins to the right. South of the equator, it spins left. This *Coriolis effect* is caused by the earth's rotation. Water, wind, and even objects like thrown baseballs, all spin slightly right in the Northern Hemisphere. They spin left in the Southern Hemisphere.

The Coriolis effect decides which way water currents flow and winds blow. And the wind plays one of the biggest roles in the movement of the sea.

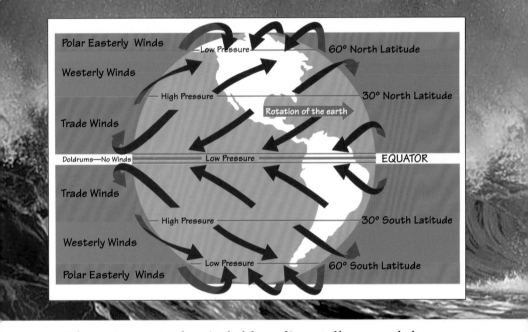

The constant trade winds blow diagonally toward the equator. They push the sea westward. Then the Coriolis effect takes over. At higher **latitudes**, the wind curves, pushing the ocean east again. This giant circle of surface currents is called a *gyre*.

CURRENTS

Who cares about currents? Everyone does, although they may not know it.

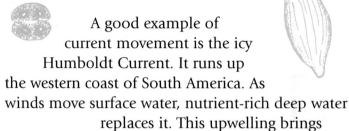

A good example of current movement is the icy Humboldt Current. It runs up the western coast of South America. As winds move surface water, nutrient-rich deep water 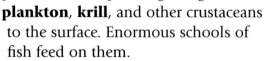 replaces it. This upwelling brings **plankton**, **krill**, and other crustaceans to the surface. Enormous schools of fish feed on them.

These fish support both the Peruvian fishing industry and large populations of seabirds. The bird droppings, or *guano*, are harvested for fertilizer.

But every few years, the winds refuse to blow. The upwelling stops. Fish die. Birds starve. Fishing fleets cannot fill their nets. The fertilizer industry closes down. The Peruvian people pray for the winds to come again.

In short, one way or another, all life on Earth depends on the sea.

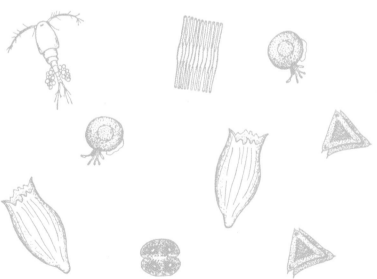

AN ALIEN LANDSCAPE

Suns, moons, planets, asteroids, comets, and meteors
are found in outer space. But what do you know about
inner space? More men have walked on the moon than on
the bottom of the ocean. In fact, humans have not yet seen
95 percent of this alien land.

Pretend you're at the seashore. You're watching waves. Beneath the whitecaps lies an underwater ledge. This **continental shelf** slopes gently down to about 600 feet.

Continental shelves edge nearly all coastlines. In most places, the shelves stretch about 40 miles out to sea. But the one off Siberia extends 800 miles into the Arctic Ocean.

In a few places, the shelves don't exist at all. Currents in these places flow swiftly. **Sediment** that forms the shelves can't collect.

The shelves drop off into a steeper zone. These are the **continental slopes**. If you could sled some of these slopes, you'd end up 12,000 feet underwater.

At the bottom of the slopes, you'd find the **continental rises**. These gradual inclines give way to the flat plains of the deep ocean floor.

Now picture big mountains, towering above desert sand. Sink those mountains two miles underwater. You'll see the **midocean ridges**. Underwater mountain chains snake through all the oceans. The system is 45,000 miles long and hundreds of miles wide.

How big were the mountains you pictured? The Mid-Atlantic Range cuts the Atlantic Ocean in half. This range is over 10,000 feet tall. And it covers more area than the Himalayas. The East Pacific Rise is found in the Pacific Ocean. It stretches 6,000 miles from the Gulf of California to Antarctica.

Both ranges have deep channels between their ridges. These troughs, crisscrossed with cracks, are called **fracture zones**. The Mid-Atlantic's trough is 15 miles wide and 4 miles deep. That's four times deeper than the Grand Canyon.

In places such as the Red Sea and the Gulf of California, the ridge system butts against the continents. These regions rock and roll with earthquakes and volcanoes.

Most midocean ridges are, in fact, underwater volcanoes. Called **seamounts**, they play an important part in our planet's **plate tectonics**. *Tectonics* comes from the Greek word *tekton*. It means "to build." In this case, it means the building of the earth's crust. The plates are a fairly recent discovery.

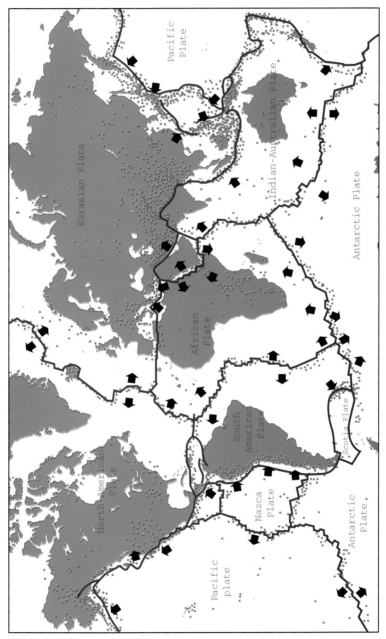

This map shows the plates in the earth's crust. Scientists named the plates. Much of the United States sits on the North American plate. Arrows show how experts think the plates are moving. The red dots show where earthquakes have occurred.

To understand how plate tectonics works, let's look at the earth's structure. In the center is the core. The temperature there is about 12,000°F! The heat radiates outward and travels in circles. As the heat moves round and round, rock melts. This inner layer of molten rock is called the **mantle**.

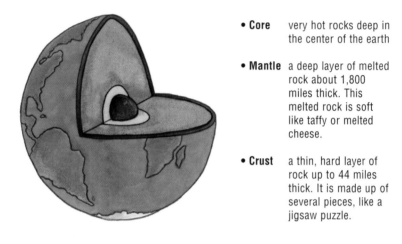

- **Core**   very hot rocks deep in the center of the earth

- **Mantle**   a deep layer of melted rock about 1,800 miles thick. This melted rock is soft like taffy or melted cheese.

- **Crust**   a thin, hard layer of rock up to 44 miles thick. It is made up of several pieces, like a jigsaw puzzle.

The mantle rises. It cools as it nears the surface and hardens again. This layer is called **crust**. It's the earth's shell. The crust is like an eggshell under pressure. Millions of years ago, the earth's crust cracked and broke into pieces. The pieces are called *plates*.

Beneath the plates, the hot mantle churns slowly. The plates floating on top move too. They often bump into neighboring plates. Sometimes they bounce apart. Other times, one pushes under another one.

This bumping and pushing causes intense **seismic activity**. Think of dinner plates, sliding into one another. When they hit, *crash*! When crustal plates hit, *kerthunk*! Earthquakes occur.

In the Atlantic, the continents rest on plates that were once joined. Now they're moving apart, about an inch per year. That's about as fast as fingernails grow.

As they move apart, the Mid-Atlantic Range forms new crust to fill in the gaps. **Magma** bubbles up from inside the trough. It spills over the sides, spreads out, and hardens. This spreading means the Atlantic seafloor is growing wider.

But growth in the Atlantic means that the Pacific is shrinking. The plates there move too. But they don't bounce apart. They overlap, forcing the edge of one under the edge of another. This does two things. It makes mountains grow. And it forms deep underwater trenches as crust is drawn down into the mantle. There the crust remelts, starting the cycle over again. This is called *subduction*.

Deep sea trenches surround the Pacific Basin. They have an average depth of 4½ miles. The Mariana Trench, east of the Philippines, is 7 miles deep. It's the lowest point on Earth.

Almost 600 active volcanoes rise above the Pacific trenches. They are fed by crust that returns to the mantle to become magma. Most volcanoes erupt well beneath the waves. This circle of volcanoes is called the "Ring of Fire."

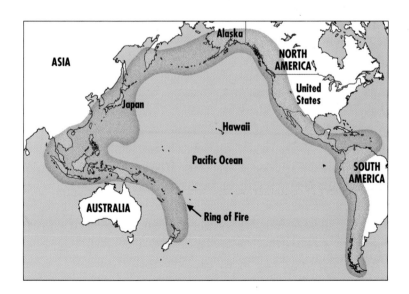

Did you know nearly all islands started out as undersea volcanoes? As they erupted over and over, rocks piled taller and taller. When the peaks poked above the surface, they became islands.

Some places such as Hawaii are strings of islands. They were formed by plates, rotating above stationary volcanoes.

Volcanic islands are numerous above the Pacific plate. Rising more than 30,000 feet above the seafloor, they are the tallest mountains in the world.

Most people think Mt. Everest is the tallest mountain in the world. Sorry. That record goes to Mauna Kea. The Hawaiian volcano rises 33,476 feet from seafloor to peak. Everest tops out just over 29,000 feet.

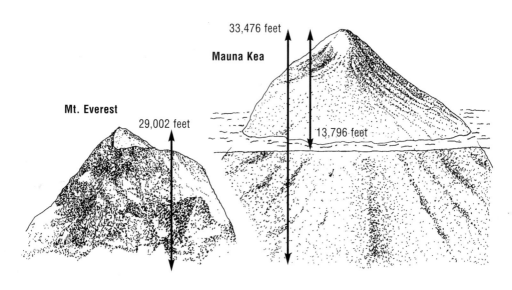

Mountains, taller than Everest. Canyons, deeper than the Grand Canyon. Trenches, even deeper than that. Volcanoes, recycling the earth's crust as magma. Inner space is a fascinating and slightly scary place.

And if it seems a little scary now, centuries ago it was simply terrifying.

chapter 3

SOUNDING THE DEPTHS

Most of what we know about the ocean we've learned in the last few decades. The ocean is such a big part of our world. So why did it take us so long? Fear of the unknown was the major obstacle.

For a long time, people believed the earth was flat. Who wanted to sail off the edge of the world? Oh, a few brave souls challenged the sea. But many never returned home. Fierce storms and wicked waves sunk ships and drowned men.

And that was just on the surface of the water. What horrible dangers lurked below? What hungry monsters lay in wait? From time to time, odd sea creatures washed ashore. As they arose from the depths, myths and **superstitions** arose too. Men of science decided to put such fears to rest.

Henry the **Navigator** (1394–1460) was a Portuguese prince. In 1415, Henry established the first European school of navigation at Sagres, Portugal. He recruited mathematicians, chart makers, astronomers, and ships' captains.

Together, they designed ships, drew charts, and studied the stars. They improved navigational equipment such as compasses and **quadrants**. A new generation of explorers received instruction at the school. Vasco da Gama and Christopher Columbus studied at Sagres. Later, Ferdinand Magellan studied at the school.

In 1519, Magellan set out to sail around the globe. It was a dangerous journey. He left Spain with 280 men. Only 18 returned. Magellan himself was killed in the Philippines.

Vasco da Gama

Christopher Columbus

Magellan was a brave explorer. But he wasn't much of a scientist. After sailing west around southern South America, Magellan found a quiet ocean. He named the ocean *Pacific,* meaning "peaceful."

Magellan wondered how deep it was. So he decided to **sound** it.

Ferdinand Magellan

Magellan spliced together some ropes and attached them to a cannonball. Then he dropped it overboard.

The cannonball dropped 400 fathoms, or 2,400 feet. Magellan never felt the ball hit bottom. So he declared the ocean "bottomless."

Of course, we know that isn't so. But later soundings also proved incorrect. Often, the weight hit so gently no one noticed the rope jerk. So the line kept uncoiling. That led to false depth readings up to 11 miles. That's more than 1½ times the actual distance to the deepest point of the seafloor.

By the mid-1800s, accuracy increased. Better equipment helped. The need to find the best routes for undersea telegraph cables also helped.

At the time, people thought the Atlantic ocean floor was a flat, barren plain. Imagine their surprise when depth soundings showed hills and valleys. And where they thought the ocean should have been the deepest, they found a rise. It was named Telegraph Plateau. It seemed the perfect place to lay cable.

Then Charles Darwin stunned the world with his book *The Origin of Species*. His theory of evolution sent scientists scampering to find living **fossils**. The ocean floor seemed the perfect lair for **trilobites**, sea scorpions, and other prehistoric beasts.

Exploratory ships headed out. Dredges and scoop nets went down to depths up to 3 miles. Scientists found no trilobites. But they did discover an amazing assortment of animals. Some, indeed, were related to ancient species.

Sea lilies looked like plants with long stalks and petals. But they were actually animals. Their "petals" were arms that fished food from the water. Their ancestors had thrived 100 million years ago when dinosaurs stalked the earth.

Every haul brought unique discoveries. Up came glass sponges. These were named for the clear **filaments** that attached them to the ocean floor. Brittle stars and sea pens with feathery arms that looked like writing quills were found. Bouquets of animals with stalks like plants glowed pale purple.

Illustration from Jules Verne's
Twenty Thousand Leagues Under the Sea

In 1871, Jules Verne's *Twenty Thousand Leagues Under the Sea* was a big hit. Verne's tale of undersea adventure made people curious. Could humans truly travel 20,000 leagues beneath the ocean's surface? Did monsters like giant squid really exist?

A year later, England's H.M.S. *Challenger* set sail. She had one goal. That was to study the sea. For nearly four years, her crew charted every ocean but the Arctic. They dredged. They probed. They scooped and netted. They paved the way for future inquiring minds.

Careful soundings brought new understanding of the seafloor. The *Challenger* team discovered continental shelves and midocean ridges. They found trenches over 5 miles deep. Could that be right? they wondered. So they measured again—just to make sure.

Inside the *Challenger*

Near the Canary Islands, the crew brought up rocks that looked like coal. The scientists thought they were fossils or **meteorites**. Later research discovered that the rocks were mainly **manganese**. The earth's largest manganese deposits lie 16,000 feet below the surface of the Pacific!

The rocks also contained iron, nickel, zinc, cobalt, and other valuable metals. In the center of each rock was an object such as a shark's tooth or a whale bone. The metals clung to them in layers, growing like pearls around a grain of sand.

Challenger researchers knew this deep environment must be pitch black and very cold. But they never guessed the oversized treasures their nets would reveal. Giant worms and slugs were pulled in with crabs and prawns with incredibly long legs. Shrimp grew as big as lobsters.

The sea lilies, sponges, and multicolored, **fluorescent** creatures had never been seen before. In fact, the scientists netted 4,717 new species. The ocean bottom wasn't dead at all. It swarmed with life!

How did these bottom-dwellers feed? The answer lay in the sediment hauled aboard. It was full of tiny skeletons and shells from plankton. As these microscopic plants and animals died, they fell to the bottom.

Remember the food chain? This constant cycle creates an **organic** "snow." The tiny plants and animals tumble downward by the ton to feed scavengers on the ocean floor. These, in turn, are eaten by predators such as giant squid.

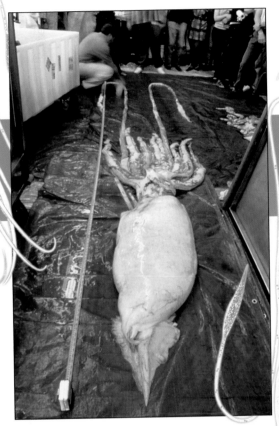

Oh, yes, giant squid do exist. In 1873, fishermen found one off the coast of Newfoundland. It put up quite a fight before it escaped, missing two legs. One of them measured 19 feet long. Later catches proved the giant squid to be about 60 feet long. It is the planet's biggest invertebrate. But even today, we don't know much about this monster of the deep.

The *Challenger* expedition did not find all the answers—or all the secrets—of the ocean's farthest reaches. But they did discover that no matter how deep, no matter how dark, life finds a way to survive and even thrive.

THE CHALLENGE OF THE DEEP

The *Challenger* proved that life existed deep down in the ocean. Some areas were filled with it. Others seemed to have only a few worms or sponges. Why the difference? Dredging and netting didn't offer many answers. Some of the creatures *Challenger* hauled aboard looked like goo. To learn more, people had to dive.

The very first divers were probably hungry. Over 4,000 years ago, Indians dived deep for mussels off the coast of Peru. The sea was full of good things to eat, some of them deep underwater.

About the same time, clear across the world in the Gulf of

Arabia, men were diving for oysters. They may have eaten them. But they also wanted the pearls lodged inside their shells.

Those guys could really hold their breath! Their only gear were stone weights to make them sink really fast. The men worked fast too. They only had a couple of minutes until their lungs ran out of air.

To stay underwater longer, divers needed to take air with them. So why not just run a tube to the surface like a long snorkel?

Pressure was the biggest challenge of diving deep. Water is heavy stuff!

On the beach, the weight of air pressing against your body is about 15 pounds per square inch. Now get into the water and dive. As you go down, each foot of water above you increases the pressure by about ½ a pound. At 100 feet deep, every square inch of your body feels an extra 50 pounds of pressure. It pushes from all sides, squeezing you like a balloon.

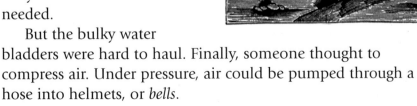

Your air supply must have the same pressure as the water around you. If you tried breathing through a pipe to the surface, water pressure would squeeze the air from your lungs.

Over 2,000 years ago, Greek sponge divers invented simple **scuba** gear. Water bladders were made from animal skins. They were oiled to make them waterproof. Then the bladders were inflated. Divers could then carry air and use it when needed.

But the bulky water bladders were hard to haul. Finally, someone thought to compress air. Under pressure, air could be pumped through a hose into helmets, or *bells*.

Fill a big jar or bowl with water. Now turn a clear drinking glass upside down. Push it straight down into the water. See how air stays in the glass, keeping the water out? That's a simple bell.

Diving bells aren't modern inventions. Aristotle (383–322 B.C.) described bells that let sponge divers breathe underwater. Alexander the Great (356–323 B.C.) used a primitive diving bell for battle. History doesn't mention bells again until 1531. Then, near Rome, they were used to search for treasure.

Those early bells relied on the air captured within them. When the pocket was used up, the diver had to return to the surface. It usually took about an hour to reach the surface.

In 1715, self-contained diving gear appeared. Airtight leather suits provided some insulation against cold seawater. Metal helmets had windows. Tubes provided fresh air and carried away carbon dioxide. With weights, divers could walk and work on the seafloor. At least in fairly shallow water.

In 1717, British astronomer Edmund Halley built a more practical diving bell. It was made of wood, with windows at the top for light. Air came in through leather tubes. The tubes were connected to barrels of air. Halley's system was "state of the art" for 70 years.

The main problem was with the hoses. Often, they tangled. Sometimes they broke. If that happened, *whoosh!* The air rushed from the diver's helmet. The squeeze caused by the loss of air pressure almost always killed the diver.

A fix was a long time coming. More than two centuries, in fact.

You may have heard of the man who changed diving forever. His name was Jacques Cousteau. He graduated from a French naval academy in 1933. He wanted to become a pilot. But that didn't happen.

The fiery Frenchman almost died in an auto accident. While recovering, he discovered diving. It became his passion. His love for the sport inspired him to improve it. Cousteau teamed with engineer Emile Gagnon. Together

Jacques Cousteau demonstrating the Aqua Lung—1950

they designed the **Aqua Lung**. *Aqua* is the Latin word for "water." The "lung" was a metal bottle. It was strapped to a diver's back.

This is the scuba gear you have probably seen. Safety valves deliver just the right amount of air. And just the right pressure is maintained. Now divers could go deeper and stay down longer. This led to new challenges.

As early scuba divers went down, some felt dizzy, even downright goofy. They did dumb things. Some removed their mouthpieces and tried to breathe water. This strange behavior was called *narcosis*. It was caused by too much nitrogen in the brain.

Excess nitrogen also caused a painful condition called *the bends*. When divers breathed compressed air, nitrogen passed through the walls of their lungs. It dissolved in the blood and built up in tissues.

Everything was fine as long as the divers stayed below, under pressure. But if they came up fast, the nitrogen caused bubbles to form in the blood and tissues.

EXPERIMENT

Grab a bottle of soda and look at it. Carbon dioxide is dissolved in the soda. It stays there, under pressure, as long as the cap is on. Twist off that cap. What happened? The pressure is reduced. Carbon dioxide bubbles up inside the soda.

That's what happened to divers. As they came to the surface, the pressure lessened. Nitrogen bubbles formed. Bubbles in the brain or spine sometimes produced paralysis, numbness, speech defects, or nausea. Bubbles in the joints caused severe pain. Sometimes the divers couldn't straighten them. That's where the term *the bends* came from.

The problem had a simple solution. Divers had to come up slowly so nitrogen could escape without bubbling. This gradual decrease of pressure is called *decompression*. It worked, but it took a long time. If divers stayed 300 feet deep for 1 hour, they would have to spend 7½ hours rising to the surface!

Scientists looked for a way to shorten this time. They knew people needed oxygen. But what if they mixed it with something besides nitrogen? Could they use helium? It didn't dissolve easily in blood.

A mixture of oxygen, helium, and just a bit of nitrogen worked perfectly. It shortened decompression and solved the narcosis problem. Now scuba divers can safely explore about 400 feet down. A few have gone even deeper, using special equipment.

Steve Etchemendy is director of marine operations at the Monterey Bay Aquarium Research Institute (MBARI). He holds the world record for working dives—1,780 feet. He did it in a JIM suit. This armored diving gear looks like a space suit.

"Most deepwater diving is oil field work," Etchemendy explained. "Stuff like cleaning undersea wellheads. That's what I was doing when I set my world record."

Growing up, Etchemendy wanted to be an astronaut. But at 12, he had to get glasses. Astronauts need perfect vision. "So I decided to follow Cousteau's footsteps and become an aquanaut," he said.

Besides the JIM suit, Etchemendy often uses an atmospheric diving suit. The bullet-shaped metal suit is nicknamed WASP because it looks like one. Out of the water, the suit is so heavy that a crane has to lift it.

But in the water, the suit "flies" with the greatest of ease. The pilot's feet work propellers that let him move up, down, forward, backward, left, or right. His arms slide into sleeves, tipped with steel claws. A large, dome-shaped "windshield" gives him a wide-angle view. WASP suits are pressurized and work to about 1,700 feet deep.

WASP suit

WASP suit

In the abyss, water pressure reaches 7 tons per square inch. Sea creatures are made mostly of water. That's why they don't crush. But hollow objects like metal suits tend to collapse under such immense pressure.

The deep poses other challenges. Seawater is **corrosive** like acid. Salt chews at things. It is also thick and opaque. Sunlight can only penetrate a few hundred feet into the ocean. After that, the water dims to a blue-black darkness.

And the temperature plunges. In places, the water is below 32°F. Remember, saltwater freezes at a lower temperature than freshwater. So saltwater can be very cold without being frozen.

To overcome such obstacles, deepwater travelers need special vehicles.

chapter

DEEPWATER VEHICLES

Imagine underwater vehicles. Chances are you think of submarines. Like many great inventions, submarines were designed for war. You probably knew that. But did you know the first submarine went for a cruise in 1620?

The first sub was built by inventor Cornelius Drebbel. It had a wooden hull. It was covered with leather and waterproofed with **tallow**. It had no motor, only oars. They came out of the hull through watertight leather joints.

Drebbel test-drove his sub in the Thames River in England. It worked! So he built a larger one. Neither went below 15 feet deep. But they did go 4 miles per hour.

Over the next decade, Drebbel's subs made daily trips in the Thames. People came from all over Europe to watch. Thousands took rides, including King James I.

Cornelius Drebbel

Drebbel tried to sell his invention as a lean, mean war machine. But the British navy was not impressed.

The first submarine used for warfare was built by American David Bushnell. In 1776, the Revolutionary War was close at hand. British warships had set sail. But America had no navy to fight the British. General George Washington liked the idea of an underwater weapon.

Bushnell's *Turtle* looked like a giant wooden barrel. It had **ballast** tanks and propellers, but no motor. The propellers were cranked by hand. The *Turtle* cruised just beneath the surface. A **conning tower** poked out of the water. The driver looked through a little porthole while he steered. When necessary, the sub could go completely underwater.

The idea was to use the sub to sneak up on British warships. Then the driver could attach explosives to the warships and beat a hasty retreat. The *Turtle* sneaked up on a ship or two, but never blew up any. After being spotted by the British, the sub was retired. A secret weapon is only useful as long as it stays secret.

Bushnell's submarine

The first sub to sink an enemy ship was the C.S.S. *Hunley*. She fought on the Confederate side in America's Civil War. Carrying dynamite on her bow, the *Hunley* set off to sink the Yankee ship *Housatonic*. The charge went off early. Both sub and ship went down.

Like the *Turtle*, the *Hunley* attacked in the **awash** position. But the crew didn't like to go underwater because they worried about air.

Once a reliable air supply was developed, subs could stay under longer. And they could go deeper. By 1900, they regularly cruised 100 feet deep.

After that, they improved quickly due to the two world wars. The superpowers (Germany, England, and the United States) understood the important role subs could play. By the end of World War II, subs operated at depths of 800 feet.

In 1963, America introduced a brand-new attack sub, the *Thresher*. At the time, the United States and Russia perched on the brink of nuclear war. The *Thresher*, and others like her, were to be the front line of defense against the Soviets' growing fleet.

The nuclear-powered *Thresher* was built for **stealth**, not speed. Her superthick hull allowed her to dive 1,300 feet, deeper than any other sub. And special silencing equipment hid the noise of her engines and gears. This sub was deep and quiet. It was dynamite! Everyone thought she'd blow the others out of the water!

Thresher

But on April 10, 1963, the *Thresher* mysteriously sank off the coast of Nova Scotia. Her entire crew of 129 men went down with her.

President Kennedy sent condolences. But the crew's families wanted an explanation. The navy had none. The newspapers asked why there was no rescue attempt. Again, the navy had no answers.

In the wake of the disaster, the navy scrambled to build Deep Submergence Rescue Vehicles (DSRVs). The pair, called *Mystic* and *Avalon*, could rescue 24 people at a time from sunken submarines. But they would be years away.

Meanwhile, subs, ships, and men searched for the *Thresher*. After many months,

President Kennedy

they hadn't found a clue. She'd simply vanished somewhere in water 1½ miles deep. No other submarine at that time could follow her that deep.

The situation called for a different kind of vessel. Something able to withstand the challenges of the deep. The navy had retired a suitable craft only a few years before. The guys in charge of the rescue called for the *Trieste*.

chapter

SEVEN MILES DEEP

In the early 1900s, William Beebe was **curator** at the New York Zoological Gardens. The ocean's middle region especially fascinated him. He'd done a lot of research off the eastern seaboard. But he wanted better ways to learn about creatures of the deep.

In 1930, Beebe teamed up with engineer Otis Barton. They built a deepwater vehicle. Beebe called it a *bathysphere*. *Bathos* is Greek for "deep." A *sphere* is a ball.

William Beebe

The bathysphere was a steel ball. It was less than 5 feet across. Its round shape helped it resist water pressure, which pushed evenly all around. Two men could barely fit inside. That meant less hollow space.

A cable and **winch** lowered and raised the craft. The heavy steel **tether** was its biggest drawback. It was firmly attached to the mother ship. The bathysphere hung from the tether. The tiny ball was at the mercy of waves on the surface. Big swells made for a wild ride.

Beebe and Barton could barely squeeze through the 14-inch wide entrance. It had a thick steel door and three 6-inch windows made of quartz. Two had been installed at the factory. But Beebe wanted a third. He asked his crew to put it in. It was a good thing he test-drove the craft.

The scientist lowered the unmanned bathysphere to 3,000 feet. It came up full of water—pressurized water. Beebe started to loosen the door bolts.

"After the first few turns," he wrote in his book *Half Mile Down*, "a strange, high singing came forth. Then a fine mist . . . shot out, a needle of steam. Then another and another."

Beebe realized the danger and cleared the deck. Little by little, he turned one of the brass bolts. Suddenly, it shot across the deck "like a shell from a gun." The bolt burrowed into a solid steel winch, 30 feet away. Water, fueled by the pressure of the deep, jetted from the bathysphere.

But that didn't stop Beebe and Barton. They worked out the bugs.

Finally, it was time to give the bathysphere a try. The two men crowded inside the little ball. The crew sealed the door. Think how the scientists felt!

What if the bathysphere leaked? What if the winch couldn't lift them with all that water between them and the ship? What if the pressure crushed them like nutshells?

Down they went anyway. They dropped to over 1,000 feet. They had entered a world no man could have imagined. Blue. Deep blue. Black-blue. According to Beebe, "Yellow and orange and red were unthinkable. The blue which filled all space admitted no thought of other colors."

And yet, what a light show! Fish, jellyfish, and animals appeared that Beebe couldn't even name. One was bigger than the bathysphere. It had huge eyes and light-producing fangs. Long tentacles, tipped with flashing red and blue lights, lured prey into its wide jaws. Beebe later categorized the creature as a sea dragon.

Over the next four years, the bathysphere made 35 dives. On August 15, 1934, Beebe and Barton took the ride of a lifetime. Down they dropped. They were suspended at 3,028 feet. This deep-diving record stood for 15 years.

But the two men only stayed five minutes. Beebe was thrilled. His spotlight awoke the absolute darkness. A jellyfish floated by. Something very large swam after it.

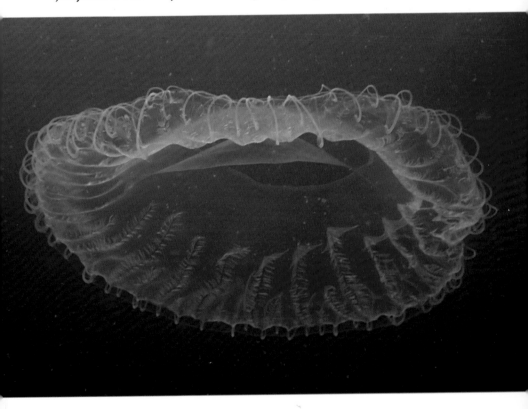

"Twenty feet," he wrote, "is the least possible estimate I can give to its full length." Later, he guessed the creature was a whale. Or maybe it was a whale shark.

As Beebe journeyed down, Auguste Piccard was going up. Way up. The Swiss scientist loved to invent and explore. Curious about cosmic rays, he invented a balloon.

The FNRS-1 balloon had a pressurized gondola. Inside, observers breathing bottled oxygen could climb to altitudes thought impossible. In 1931, Piccard rose to 53,000 feet. That's twice as high as man had gone before. High enough to reach the stratosphere. The following year, he and his twin brother, Jean, reached 55,000 feet.

Piccard met Beebe at the 1933 World's Fair in Chicago. When he learned about the deep, he wanted to see it himself. And when he heard about the bathysphere, he decided to improve it.

By 1948, Piccard's bathyscaphe was ready to test dive. The FNRS-2 borrowed its design—and name—from Piccard's balloon. It was bigger than Beebe's machine. It had thicker steel walls. Plexiglas ports allowed wide-angle viewing.

The tether was gone. No more bouncing along with the mother ship. No more worries about winches and cables. Instead, the passenger cabin hung beneath a huge upper tank filled with gasoline. Since gas is lighter than water, the FNRS-2 floated.

To go down, two chambers in the upper tank were filled with water. That made the craft just heavy enough to sink. To go back up, pellets of iron ballast were released. Minus the extra weight, the bathyscaphe floated to the surface.

The unmanned FNRS-2 went down 4,554 feet. But the test dive uncovered problems—expensive problems. Still Piccard found the funding to build a bigger, better model. He named it *Trieste*.

The *Trieste* first took the plunge in 1953, off the coast of Naples. Finally, it was judged safe for people. So Piccard and his son Jacques climbed in. Down they went, almost two miles. *Bump*! They hit bottom. Outside, in the spotlight, they saw—

Not much. No spectacular light shows. No undersea mountains or erupting volcanoes. They saw nothing but a flat, muck-covered plain. The people who had funded Piccard's *Trieste* expected much more. Disappointed, they backed out.

But the United States Navy wanted new ideas for underwater warfare. In 1957, they signed a contract with Piccard. The Office of Naval Research (ONR) would fund 15 dives. Half of them would study sound movement through the sea.

The *Trieste* took scientists deeper than ever before. She carried and placed **hydrophones**. These underwater microphones became part of the Navy's Sound Surveillance System. They were used to spy on Soviet subs.

Beyond that, the *Trieste* opened the door to a bold, new world. The array of deepwater life surprised biologists. Shrimp, eels, and eerily lit unknowns flitted past the portals. Tripod fish used their superlong fins like "landing gears" and *boinged* like grasshoppers. Rat-tail fish hunted in inky waters using sensitive antennae.

Geologists analyzed seafloor sediment. They learned much about the beginnings of our planet. Robert Dietz of the Navy Electronics Lab in San Diego made new discoveries about the plate tectonics theory.

In 1958, the ONR bought the *Trieste* and ordered immediate improvements. Jacques Piccard stayed on as a consultant.

On January 23, 1960, Piccard and Navy Lieutenant Don Walsh climbed into the new, improved *Trieste*. The seas off Guam were stormy that morning. Piccard and Walsh were nervous. But not because of the weather. You see, the two were about to go to the very bottom of the world.

Down they went for five hours. They bumped to a stop. The men were almost 7 miles down in the Challenger Deep, the deepest hole in the Mariana Trench. And at 35,800 feet, it's the deepest spot on our planet.

Yet even there, they found life. A fish, something like a **sole**, swam through the ooze. Oddly, considering its lightless habitat, it had eyes. There were shrimp and tiny invertebrates. The men saw life in those greatest depths! That meant oxygen. Currents must carry it down from above. What a discovery!

Despite her success, the *Trieste* retired in 1961. She did come out of mothballs to find *Thresher*'s remains. But what she found wasn't a pretty picture. Deep-sea pressure had twisted the sub into metal pretzels.

The navy knew they had to learn more about the abyss. They could not use the *Trieste*. She did well using up and down movements. Much else was beyond her scope.

A much different design was needed to really explore the deep.

chapter 7

THE NEW WAVE

WOODS HOLE

The new **submersibles** were smaller and streamlined. They looked more like boats than like balls. And who do you think built the first one? Not General Dynamics that built submarines for the navy. And it wasn't Lockheed that built later subs.

Charles Momsen

Would you believe it was General Mills? That's right, the cereal company. *Alvin* was born in 1964 surrounded by Cheerios.

The little sub was the brainchild of the ONR's Charles Momsen.

Three people could ride inside. Each had a small window. Gone was the huge gasoline tank. A new foam invention provided lift. Cruising depth was 6,000 feet.

Alvin was named for Allyn (Al) Vine, a scientist at the Woods Hole Oceanographic Institute. Woods Hole on Cape Cod would be the sub's home. No one else wanted her. That is, not until she proved herself.

It didn't take long. *Alvin* wasn't built to withstand the Challenger Deep. She was built for speed and easy handling. Those were her strengths.

Not long after, a fleet of look-alikes and knockoffs were introduced. But *Alvin* remains the submersible queen. Yes, she still roams the ocean today. Remodeled and rebuilt, she can now go 15,000 feet deep. She has traveled around the world and made over 3,000 dives.

The *Titanic*

Alvin has searched for everything from whales to wrecked ships. In 1985, she played a key role in locating the *Titanic*. The sunken ocean liner lay hiding in over 12,000 feet of water.

The little sub had help from *Jason Jr.*, a Remotely Operated Vehicle (ROV). ROVs "see" with cameras and "hear" with **sonar**. Then they pass that information along to scientists who are watching monitors. ROVs also have arms with claws for lifting things.

The *Titanic* mission was directed by Dr. Robert Ballard. Ballard, a scientist at Woods Hole, had piloted *Alvin* many times. He discovered the *Titanic* and the sunken battleships *Bismarck* and *Yorktown*. Then Ballard's focus turned to deep-sea archeology.

Why does he find this new frontier so exciting? In 1997, a navy sub went looking for a lost Israeli submarine. It didn't find the *Dakar* then. But its sonar suggested another shipwreck.

Ballard went to the scene with *Jason* (*Jason Jr.*'s big brother). The ROV scanned the depths with sonar and cameras.

After several hours, *Jason* found not one shipwreck, but two. They were stuck in mud over 1,000 feet down in the Mediterranean Sea. Above the seafloor, both ships had rotted away. But beneath the mud, they were beautifully preserved.

Ballard analyzed the artifacts *Jason* retrieved. They dated back to 750 B.C. Their origin was Phoenician. The Phoenicians lived in what is now Lebanon from 1200 B.C. to about 146 B.C. They were seafaring traders. The sunken ships were probably carrying wine to Egypt or Carthage.

Ballard said the Phoenicians were the "greatest sailors . . . extremely brave and adventurous. To find one of their ships is to touch that history."

Ancient history, yes. Yet not as ancient as Ballard's 1999 discovery. While searching for shipwrecks in the Black Sea, the scientist uncovered evidence of Noah's biblical flood. Sonar found the outline of what once was a beach. But it was 550 feet underwater.

Using a dredge, Ballard collected some shells from the undersea beach. Two belonged to extinct freshwater mollusks of the preflood age. Seven were saltwater mollusks from the postflood era.

The freshwater shells were 7,500 years old! Both their age and the location match the Old Testament story of Noah. Ballard plans to return with *Jason* to search for more clues. Meanwhile the ROV remains busy at Woods Hole.

MONTEREY BAY

Across the country in Moss Landing, California, you'll find Steve Etchemendy and MBARI. There in Monterey Bay, a huge canyon divides the continental shelf. Monterey Canyon is the largest undersea **fissure** along the entire United States coastline.

It comes very close to shore. Erosion brings it ever closer. The old Moss Landing pier used to be twice as long. But the tip keeps falling into Monterey Canyon.

Just beyond the bay, the canyon splits. Its deepest part is over 2 miles deep. Its size, shape, and location increase nutrient flows to the area. These flows maintain a wide web of sea life.

A huge floating forest of kelp feeds shellfish such as mussels, clams, and abalone. They, in turn, lure anchovies, rockfish, tuna, and salmon to the area. Then they become food for sharks, squid, sea lions, and whales.

Oh, and seabirds! Millions of them hover over the bay.

Altogether, Monterey's rich midwater region supports 300 kinds of fish, 100 kinds of birds, and a host of marine mammals. MBARI's 14 primary investigators (PIs) explore the area regularly.

"The largest portion of the earth's living 'stuff' is in the midwater zone of the ocean," explained Etchemendy. "There's more of it there than anywhere!"

Etchemendy once worked at Woods Hole. He piloted *Alvin* for four years. Now he's hot on ROVs. MBARI houses two. The *Ventana* (Spanish for "window") is an older model.

"She's **hydraulic**," said Etchemendy, "and very strong. *Ventana* drills holes for seismic equipment and takes water samples."

She also captures animals and sucks them into holding

tanks for further study. MBARI scientists find at least 12 new species every year.

Ventana is fast. But she's so noisy that she scares away the animals she's trying to catch. MBARI built Tiburon especially for its research. Her name is Spanish for "shark."

Tiburon can go four times deeper than Ventana. According to Etchemendy, "She's electric, very quiet. She doesn't affect her environment, which is important for certain types of research. Both ROVs play vital roles in our work here at MBARI."

photo by: Greg Pio for MBARI ©1997

There are five branches of **oceanography**. The geological branch deals with rocks and sediment. The biological branch studies the sea's plants and animals. Water is analyzed by chemical oceanographers. They want to know about its **salinity**, nutrients, and pollutants.

Geophysical oceanographers are concerned with earthquakes, tectonics, and similar subjects. Physical oceanographers map currents and water movement.

MBARI's PIs handle four of the five. They don't chart currents. But they are especially interested in seismic activity. MBARI perches on the tremor-friendly Pacific Rim. The scientists hope someday to accurately forecast earthquakes.

JAPAN

Across the Pacific, Japan leads the way in undersea seismic research. For good reason. The southern part of that island nation sits smack on the junction of three tectonic plates. Their bump and grind accounts for $\frac{1}{10}$ of the world's earthquakes every year.

Some are monsters. In January 1999, a quake in the city of Kobe killed 5,500 people. And 142,000 died in the famous 1923 Tokyo earthquake. There's every reason to believe mega-quakes will follow. Predicting where and when could save countless lives.

The Japanese submersible *Shinkai* travels deeper than any other manned vessel in the world. On its first mission, *Shinkai* discovered deep cracks in the Pacific plate. No one had guessed they were there. Now scientists will study them to see how they contribute to the earthquake problem.

Shinkai found more than fissures. Over 20,000 feet down, she came across clams. They are the world's deepest known colony of the shellfish.

The sub also found **hydrothermal** vents. These openings in the seafloor gush water that has been superheated by magma. Despite its extreme temperature and **toxic** fumes, it's bursting with life.

chapter

THE TOUR

It's a bright June day. The breeze off the Pacific carries a pleasant chill. A big ship sways back and forth. It's waiting. On her deck sits a three-person submersible. The underwater vehicle is geared up and ready for us. The question is, are you ready to tour the abyss?

Our oceanographers have chosen a launch site off the Oregon coast. Seismic readings have shown a recent eruption of the Juan de Fuca ridge.

The ridge is 400 miles long. These underwater mountains edge the Juan de Fuca tectonic plate. It's a volcanic hot spot. It's a place where magma bubbles up to make new crust.

Juan de Fuca is a prime location for hydrothermal vents. When the plates crack to let magma out, water seeps in. It hits that melted rock, picking up minerals and heat.

Why doesn't the water boil away? Pressure! Instead, up comes a 450°F geyser with a *whoosh*! It bursts through the seafloor, carrying dissolved metals and hydrogen sulfide.

Sometimes, when the hot vent water hits cold seawater, the metals harden. They form stone chimneys of various shapes and sizes.

"Black smoker" chimneys are made of zinc, copper, and iron. Cooler "white smokers" usually contain elements like calcium and silica. Mix those with sulfur, and you can get poisonous results. Some chimney sulfides are even **radioactive**.

Chimneys grow quickly—up to 20 feet per year. Scientists found one not far off the Oregon coast. They named it Godzilla because of its monster size. This chimney was as tall as a 15-story building, or about 150 feet tall, before part of it collapsed.

What's so special about superheated geysers or poisonous chimneys? Wait and see! Right now, we're ready to begin our adventure!

As we set sail, the captain flicks a switch. *Beep, beep, beep, beep, beep.* Sonar describes the landscape beneath us. Shallow water. Flat, sandy bottom.

How does sonar work? Little pulses of sound are focused into a beam. When the beam hits something, the sound waves echo back. The time it takes for the echo to return tells how far away the object is.

Sonar was invented during World War I as a way to locate enemy subs. Oceanographers borrowed the technology to map the seafloor.

To measure depth, sound waves beam down. When they hit something beneath them, they echo back up. That tells how deep the water is. The *something* could be the ocean bottom or the top of an undersea mountain.

At first, finding ridges or valleys was hit-and-miss. Early sonar bounced a single sound wave as a ship moved forward. The echo gave a vague idea of how the bottom looked. But it was easy to overlook bumps or cracks.

Today's sonar shoots several thin beams. They spread out, like the ribs of an Oriental fan. This gives a much more precise picture of what's below.

Depth measurements are not the only way to survey the seafloor. Mapping by sonar is accurate, but not very fast. Ships travel slowly. Even using the latest sonar, it would take more than 100 years to map the entire ocean.

Scientists have found a shortcut. They use satellites. But how can something in outer space measure inner space? America's Seastat and Geostat satellites measure sea level with microwaves. Sea level is affected by **gravity**.

Gravity is stronger near undersea mountains. It attracts water, raising the sea level. The difference can be measured. For example, the water above a 7,000-foot ridge would be about 7 feet higher than average sea level.

Undersea valleys create less gravity. So the sea level above them is lower.

Satellites took less than two years to chart the whole ocean. When compared to sonar maps, the results were almost identical.

Beep, beep, beep, beep. Sonar tells us the water beneath us is now 500 feet deep. We're over a continental shelf. If we were on the East Coast, we'd have to travel about 100 miles before reaching deep water.

It's different here on the West Coast. Blame it on tectonics. With all that crustal recycling, continental shelves can't get much wider.

Remember, subduction does two things. It forms deep sea trenches. And it makes mountains grow. Anywhere a mountain rises straight up from the sea, you probably won't find a shelf at all.

Where we are, the ledge stretches about 15 miles west. Look around. See all those fishing boats? These shallow waters swarm with fish. A lot of nutrients wash into the ocean via streams and rivers. Continental shelves are like grocery stores to hungry fish.

They could also be gas stations, if fish needed such things. You may have seen the oil rigs, pumping away just off the beach. Petroleum and natural gas are buried in the continental shelves. Some of the world's wealthiest deposits are north of us in Alaska and south in the Gulf of Mexico.

Beep, beep, beep. The sonar signal changes after we pass over the continental rise. The deep water is getting even deeper. The sediment beneath us drops off steeply. Before long, the seafloor is more than a mile under our feet.

We play detective as we close in on our destination. Certain clues will tell us if we're near active hydrothermal vents. We study sensors. One scans for chemicals found near vents. Another listens for earthquakes.

We also look for a rise in water temperature. A special thermometer measures temperature changes as small as $\frac{1}{500}$ of a degree.

Why should that little bit of a temperature rise mean anything? Water has an enormous heat capacity. To raise water temperature by 1 degree takes 4,000 times more heat than to raise the temperature of the same amount of air.

Combine superheated seawater with the Coriolis effect and what do you get? If the conditions are right, an underwater tornado called a ***megaplume***.

Vent water usually spurts a few hundred feet above the seafloor. But a megaplume shoots up several thousand feet. Eventually, it cools enough to stop rising.

The Coriolis effect takes over. The megaplume starts to spin. Soon it looks like a twirling mushroom. It can grow 12 miles wide and travel hundreds of miles. And it can spin at almost 1,200 miles an hour!

The megaplume holds its shape because it's hot. Heat makes water molecules spread apart. The megaplume's water is less dense than the water around it. Fluids with different densities don't mix. So the megaplume stays together.

Scientists aren't sure exactly what makes them form. In fact, no one even knew they existed until 1986. Since then, only a handful have been seen.

Oceanographers want to know more. All that rising and spinning mixes up huge amounts of seawater. Think how much heat energy and nutrients megaplumes carry. They bring them almost to the surface.

Megaplumes travel horizontally too. Scientists wonder. Did these undersea cyclones help an odd assortment of critters colonize our planet?

Now it's time to explore the deep. So climb aboard our deepwater submersible.

chapter

INTO THE ABYSS

Down, down, down. We fall through the water quickly. But unless we look out the viewing ports, we have no sensation of movement. Outside, the water is turquoise blue. As sunlight fades, it turns deep blue. Before long, all we see is darkness—midnight-blue darkness where the sun cannot reach.

The sub hums and throbs. Oxygen in, carbon dioxide out. Sonar pulses let us know what's below.

All we can see is our gauges. They're bright green. The **bioluminescent** light show has begun outside.

Look at the colorful jellies. It's a regular parade! Big, small, all sizes in-between pass the windows. Each of them glows or pulses brightly. As we drop, the streaks of light seem to shoot up, like backward falling stars.

After an hour or so, our **altimeter** tells us we're 300 feet from bottom. Our pilot releases some steel ballast to slow our drop. Soon we're floating. At this weight, we won't go up or down.

We flip on the spotlight. Have we fallen down through the sea to land on the moon? It is, indeed, an alien landscape. Pillowy lumps of lava surround us. Here and there, cracks and craters dot the seafloor. It's hard to see very far. A drifting snow of debris clouds the water.

Our pilot radios the mother ship up on the surface. "Which way to the nearest vent?"

The scientists above can only guess. There was volcanic movement here not long ago. But hydrothermal vents only stay active so long. We get a **bearing** and hope for the best.

The pilot punches a button and we scoot across the seafloor. The sub's movement disturbs a crowd of deep-sea dwellers.

We see bright red shrimp, glass sponges, and herds of sea cucumbers. Little fish dance out of our path. Bigger ones follow. And all around we find clouds of white microbes of bacteria called *floe*.

Suddenly, the water ahead shimmers with an eerie light. "We've got a chimney!" says our pilot.

Scientists still don't know what makes chimneys glow. The one just ahead flickers like a giant undersea candle. It's a candle that exists in a sunless world of deadly gases, searing hot water, heavy metals, and extreme acidity. Surely nothing could survive in such a harsh environment. Right?

Wrong! Take a close look at the chimney. Check out the thriving community of alien life-forms. Tentacles, filaments, and threads sway in the hot water. They're attached to red-tipped tube worms, pinkish mollusks, pinto-colored fuzz, and something white that looks like noodles.

The fuzz is the key to all life in this dark, poisonous land. It's a bacteria that loves hydrogen sulfide. It is the heart of this fascinating ecosystem.

Scientists first discovered this bizarre world two decades ago. Since then, they've identified over 300 vent species. All depend on the Beggiatoa bacterium.

Some creatures, like the giant snails and clams you see, feed on the bacteria. Others, including predatory fish and giant squid, feast on the snails and clams. Still others, like tube worms, are hosts for the bacteria.

Tube worms

The bacteria lives inside the tube worms, breaking down chemicals into food.

This process is called **chemosynthesis**. Unlike most life on Earth, vent species don't rely on the sun's **photons** or **photosynthesis**. Instead, they depend on chemicals from the earth's interior. The only thing they need from above is oxygen. And seawater has plenty of that.

Many biologists now believe that Earth's very first living things were chemosynthetic too. In fact, a growing number think life on this planet began 3 billion years ago in a hydrothermal vent! It may have arrived from space on a meteor. Or it may have formed within the vent itself.

Either way, it had to travel. Remember, vents don't stay active forever. Then, as now, vent critters had to move to survive. How do they journey from place to place? Scientists aren't sure. Maybe they simply drifted on currents. Maybe megaplumes picked them up and whisked them away.

Megaplumes might explain how Beggiatoa and tube worms have taken up residence in a totally different environment. You can find both 1,000 to 2,000 feet deep on the continental rise. They need hydrogen sulfide, and there's lots of that there. Methane gas is also a need. Both are by-products of petroleum. These gases seep from the continental shelves.

The bacteria-based colonies that live in those cooler, shallower waters are called *cold-seep communities*. They function much the same as their hot-water cousins. Except some cold-seep neighborhoods cover hundreds of square miles.

Another question puzzles researchers. Why do different species flourish in different locations? You won't find giant tube worms anywhere but the Pacific. And in the Atlantic, shrimps rule!

Some oceanographers believe the species used to live together. Long ago, colonists traveled along the same ridges. With time, seafloor spreading divided the ridges and the vent communities that lived on them.

"Uh, oh," warns our pilot. "The thermometer just jumped. If the submersible gets too hot, it could mean trouble. We'd better surface."

He drops some ballast, and we start to rise. Looking back, we notice a few chimneys, leaking gray smoke. Are they about to blow? We don't wait around to find out.

It's been a fabulous trip. But it's time to go home.

chapter

WHY GO?

Climbing from the cramped submersible, we gulp fresh air. What a trip! It was great. But was it worth the expense? Why should we care about vents and their inhabitants? They're weird, all right. But what makes them special? Why do we want to know more about the world beneath the whitecaps?

Well, a wealth of minerals, such as manganese, gold, silver, copper, and oil can be found in the abyss. Scientists have found a petroleumlike oil in chimneys. It usually takes millions of years for oil to form in rocks. But inside chimneys, it only takes about 5,000 years.

Beyond minerals, we may discover new medicines. Drugs derived from vents could combat germs **resistant** to today's antibiotics. Who knows? The cure for cancer might even be down there.

Industrial cleanups are another possibility. Mining operations leave dangerous wastes behind. Sulfur, which is linked to acid rain, is one of them. Hydrogen-sulfide-eating bacteria or mussels could safely remove it. Other vent organisms might gobble up methane, copper, mercury, or cadmium. All pose health risks on land.

Steve Etchemendy believes the sea holds the answer to global warming. Most scientists agree the earth is getting warmer. The likely cause is carbon dioxide that is given off by industry and automobiles. This gas rises into the upper atmosphere and traps heat that could otherwise escape. This is called the *greenhouse effect*.

Over the last century, the earth's average temperature rose 1 degree. That isn't much. But scientists say it could rise 8 more degrees by the year 2100. What might happen then? Prolonged droughts? Horrible heat waves? Widespread crop loss and starvation?

Carbon dioxide is also absorbed by the ocean. MBARI has found elevated levels down to 2,000 feet. It's killing the coral reefs, which are home to ¼ of our planet's marine species.

So how can we slow or stop the problem? The answer may be phytoplankton, the sea's tiniest creatures.

All plants break up CO_2 into carbon and oxygen. Land plants take in the carbon and discharge oxygen. But when they die and rot, they release carbon back into the air. "They're temporary storage," explained Etchemendy.

Phytoplankton, although tiny, are the most abundant plants on Earth. They also grab carbon dioxide and release oxygen. But when they die, they fall to the seafloor. They're either eaten by bottom dwellers or become part of the sediment. They do not put carbon back up into the atmosphere.

"The ocean, which covers so much of our world, could be a great CO_2 recycling plant," said Etchemendy. "Phytoplankton could absorb ten times as much carbon dioxide as land plants."

So what's the problem? According to Etchemendy, "The Atlantic and Pacific gyres are like huge deserts in the ocean.

You won't find any phytoplankton there. There are plenty of nutrients. The only thing missing is iron."

MBARI scientists conducted an experiment near the Galapagos Islands. "We spread iron dust," said Etchemendy. "We started a huge **bloom** of phytoplankton. And all it took was 1 tablespoon of iron per acre!"

Part of the Galapagos Islands

Sounds like an easy fix, doesn't it?

"It could be an easy fix," agreed Etchemendy. "But our government doesn't spend much on researching inner space. Its focus is outer space."

Indeed, NASA is gearing up to send an ROV to Jupiter's moon Europa. The *Galileo* spacecraft has sent back photos showing interesting patterns on Europa's surface. Scientists think they point to hydrothermal vents beneath an ice-covered sea. That could mean life somewhere other than Earth.

Of course, sending a probe to Europa could have disappointing results. In January 1999, NASA launched Deep Space 2. A robotic lander touched down on Mars in December. But NASA lost contact with the expensive machine. Scientists aren't sure what happened.

Oceanographers would rather see research focus on the vast, unexplored territory right here on Earth. Why does the government hesitate? For one thing, most of the ocean belongs to no one—or to everyone.

Who has the right to minerals found in international waters? Who can legally harvest vent organisms for further study? Does anyone have the right to "take all they can" from the sea?

The 1982 United Nations Convention on the Law of the Sea (UNCLOS) treaty tried to deal with those tricky questions. But some countries, including the United States, didn't like the way it was written. It called the deep seabed "the common heritage of mankind," with profits made from it to be shared by all countries.

Finally, after much debate, the treaty came into force in late 1994. But when it speaks about the deep ocean resources, it's talking about minerals, not giant tube worms or sulfur-gulping mussels.

So what do we do about hydrothermal vents? Some people argue they should be used to replace declining resources on the earth's surface. Others say they should be left completely alone. The answer probably lies in the middle.

Research should continue. But it must be controlled so the delicate balance of vent communities is not upset. Perhaps we can create **sanctuaries** to protect them. That would keep some vents off-limits, both to research and mining.

Whatever we decide, we must decide as a worldwide community. Every government must agree on sanctuary sites and work together to see they aren't disturbed. The future of our planet may well rely on such cooperation.

Because, one way or another, all life on Earth depends on the sea.

GLOSSARY

abyss	immeasurably deep body of water
altimeter	device for measuring altitude
Aqua Lung	underwater breathing equipment
awash	covered with water
ballast	heavy material used to control the up-and-down movement of an object in the water or in the air
bearing	position in relation to another object or to a point on a compass
bioluminescent	having the ability to produce light from a living organism
bloom	excessive growth of plankton (see glossary entry)
chemosynthesis	production of organic (see glossary entry) compounds (such as living cells) using energy from chemical reactions
conning tower	raised structure on the deck of a submarine used for navigation and attack
continental rise	slight rise in the continental slope (see glossary entry) that levels off to a plain before dropping again
continental shelf	shallow underwater plain of varying width forming a border to a continent

continental slope	drop from a continental shelf (see glossary entry) to the ocean floor
corrosive	having the power to weaken or destroy gradually by chemical reaction
crust	outer layer of the earth's surface
curator	person in charge of a museum, zoo, or other place of exhibit
dorsal	situated on the back of an animal
erode	to wear away by the action of water, wind, or glacial ice
evaporate	to change from a liquid into a gas or vapor
extinction	state of no longer living
filament	a single thin flexible threadlike object
fissure	long, narrow crack in the earth's crust (see glossary entry)
fluorescent	very bright in color
fossil	trace of an organism from the past that has been preserved in the earth's crust (see glossary entry)
fracture zone	underwater area characterized by cracks
geologist	person who studies the history of the earth and its life as recorded in rocks

gravity	invisible physical force that pulls toward the center of the earth
hydraulic	operated and powered by water
hydrophone	instrument for listening to sound sent through water
hydrothermal	relating to hot water
krill	tiny animal life
latitude	invisible line of measurement north and south of the equator
magma	molten rock within the earth
manganese	grayish white metallic element that is hard and brittle
mantle	molten rock and gas that covers the earth's core
megaplume	underwater tornado
meteorite	particle of matter from outer space that reaches the surface of the earth without being vaporized
midocean ridge	underwater mountain range
navigator	person who travels over the water
oceanography	science that deals with oceans
organic	relating to or coming from living organisms
photon	unit measuring the brightness of light
photosynthesis	production of chemical compounds using energy from light

plankton	tiny plant and animal life floating or weakly swimming in a body of water
plate tectonics	science concerned with the earth's crust
quadrant	navigational instrument for measuring altitude
radioactive	showing the property of some elements to give off energetic particles or rays
resistant	having the ability to withstand the effects of something
salinity	amount of salt content
sanctuary	place of refuge or protection
scuba	underwater breathing system
sea level	level of the surface of water in relation the average level between the highest point and the lowest point
seamount	underwater mountain rising above the deep-sea floor
sediment	matter that settles to the bottom
seismic activity	vibration of the earth caused by earthquakes
sole	flatfish with a small mouth, small fins, and small eyes
sonar	method or device for locating objects underwater by means of sound waves

sound	to measure the depth of a body of water
stealth	act of moving secretly
subduction	process of the edge of one crustal plate moving below the edge of another
submersible	small underwater craft used for deep-sea research
superstition	idea held even though facts point to an opposite idea
tallow	grease from the fat of cattle and sheep
tether	cable or chain attached to something so it can't get away
toxic	poisonous
trilobite	extinct marine animal from the Paleozoic era
winch	powerful machine with a rope, cable, or chain for hauling or pulling

INDEX